What is a Dahlmanac?
An almanac is a book of
curious facts.
Roald Dahl loved curious
facts, the odder the better!
So this Dahlmanac is exactly
the kind of book Roald Dahl
would have liked.
It's got weird and wonderful
facts about amazing things like snakes
and pirates and vampires – and
lots of weird and wonderful
facts about
Roald Dahl himself!

WARNING:
Dahlmanac 2 might put
you off your breakfast.
And your lunch. Not to
mention your dinner.

Discover the gloriumptious world of
Roald Dahl

Also available on Puffin Audio

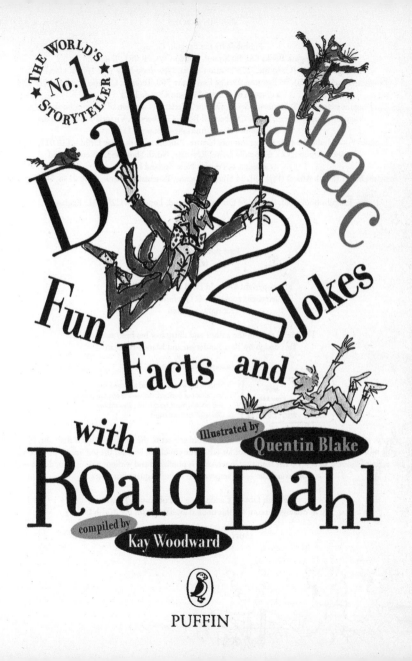

THE WORLD'S No.1 STORYTELLER

Dahlmanac

2

Fun Facts and Jokes

with

Roald Dahl

Illustrated by Quentin Blake

compiled by Kay Woodward

PUFFIN

PUFFIN BOOKS

Published by the Penguin Group
Penguin Books Ltd, 80 Strand, London WC2R 0RL, England
Penguin Group (USA) Inc., 375 Hudson Street, New York, New York 10014, USA
Penguin Group (Canada), 90 Eglinton Avenue East, Suite 700, Toronto, Ontario, Canada M4P 2Y3
(a division of Pearson Penguin Canada Inc.)
Penguin Ireland, 25 St Stephen's Green, Dublin 2, Ireland (a division of Penguin Books Ltd)
Penguin Group (Australia), 250 Camberwell Road, Camberwell, Victoria 3124, Australia
(a division of Pearson Australia Group Pty Ltd)
Penguin Books India Pvt Ltd, 11 Community Centre, Panchsheel Park, New Delhi – 110 017, India
Penguin Group (NZ), 67 Apollo Drive, Rosedale, North Shore 0632, New Zealand
(a division of Pearson New Zealand Ltd)
Penguin Books (South Africa) (Pty) Ltd, 24 Sturdee Avenue, Rosebank, Johannesburg 2196, South Africa

Penguin Books Ltd, Registered Offices: 80 Strand, London WC2R 0RL, England

puffinbooks.com

First published 2007
007

Text copyright © Roald Dahl Nominee Ltd, 2007
Illustrations copyright © Quentin Blake, 2007
All rights reserved

The moral right of the author and illustrator has been asserted
Text design by Tom Sanderson and Mandy Norman

www.greenpenguin.co.uk

British Library Cataloguing in Publication Data
A CIP catalogue record for this book is available from the British Library

ISBN: 978-0-141-32317-6

Spots

Roald Dahl loved things that made the reader go 'yuk'. Spots were just one of them. Frothing blue medicine designed to cure nasty grandmothers was another. If you're prepared to wince and squirm, then read on . . .

Other Marvellous Medicines

George isn't the only one to have invented a marvellous medicine. Check out these weird and wonderful ways of curing diseases and ailments . . .

Cooked mice were once used to treat whooping cough, smallpox and measles. They could be either roasted or fried. But if you had chickenpox, then the cure was to drink a soup made from mouse tails.

Garlic was said to cure headaches (and keep away vampires).

Cobwebs were once used to stop wounds bleeding, as well as to wrap sprains and fractures.

To get rid of bruises, a lightly beaten egg white used to be applied to the painful area.

5 Things you never knew about Roald Dahl's nose

1. His nose was nearly chopped off in an accident during his very first car journey in 1925.

2. Roald Dahl's adenoids (soft, squidgy bits at the back of the nose and throat) were mercilessly sliced out - by a doctor, of all people! - when he was eight. Worse still, the doctor didn't use anaesthetic. Ouch!

3. Roald Dahl broke his nose in a plane crash during the Second World War . . .

4. . . . but the surgeon rebuilt it in the style of a silent-film star called Rudolph Valentino, so it looked better than before.

5. His favourite smell in the whole world was that of bacon sizzling in a frying pan. Mmm . . .

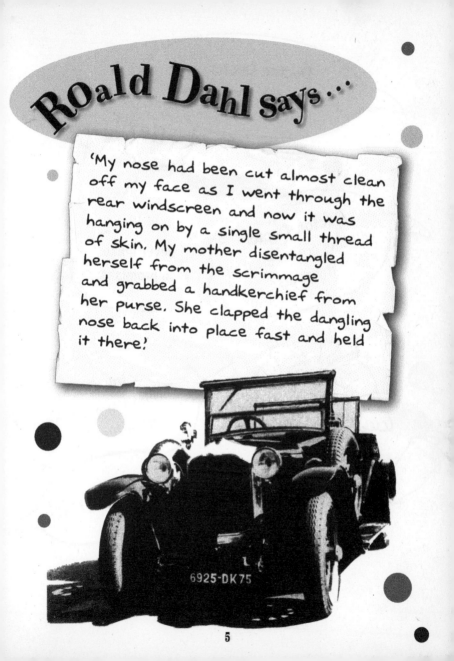

Roald Dahl says...

'My nose had been cut almost clean off my face as I went through the rear windscreen and now it was hanging on by a single small thread of skin. My mother disentangled herself from the scrimmage and grabbed a handkerchief from her purse. She clapped the dangling nose back into place fast and held it there!'

6925-DK75

Horrible illnesses
and diseases with wonderful names

Alice-in-Wonderland syndrome
Often linked with migraines, this condition makes people, animals and objects look very small indeed.

Alien-hand syndrome
People with this condition lose control of one hand. The hand acts as if it has a mind of its own.

Beriberi
Not an obsession with fruit, this is an illness caused by a lack of vitamin B1. Symptoms range from weakness and pain to death.

Ondine's curse
Sufferers have to think about every breath they take. If they do not concentrate, they stop breathing and suffocate. Falling asleep can be fatal.

Pica
This is an urge to eat things that shouldn't be eaten, such as clay, stones and even hair. Urgh.

Spotty Powder

Did you know that Roald Dahl once wrote about a miracle powder that promised to bring children out in a weird and wonderful rash of spots? Well, he did. The chapter was originally included in *Charlie and the Chocolate Factory*. But there were too many naughty children in the earlier versions of the book, so 'Spotty Powder' – and the revolting Miranda Piker – had to be dropped. Luckily, it was kept in a very safe place, so you could read it here:

'THIS stuff,' said Mr Wonka, 'is going to cause chaos in schools all over the world when I get it in the shops.'

The room they now entered had rows and rows of pipes coming straight up out of the floor. The pipes were bent over at the top and they looked like large walking sticks. Out of every pipe there trickled a stream of white crystals. Hundreds of Oompa-Loompas were running to and fro, catching the crystals in little golden boxes and stacking the boxes against the walls.

'Spotty Powder!' exclaimed Mr Wonka, beaming at the company. 'There it is! That's it! Fantastic stuff!'

'It looks like sugar,' said Miranda Piker.

'It's meant to look like sugar,' Mr Wonka said. 'And it tastes like sugar. But it isn't sugar. Oh, dear me, no.'

'Then what is it?' asked Miranda Piker, speaking rather rudely.

'That door over there,' said Mr Wonka, turning away from Miranda and pointing to a small red door at the far end of the room, 'leads directly down to the machine that makes the powder. Twice a day, I go down there myself to feed it. But I'm the only one. Nobody ever comes with me.'

They all stared at the little door on which it said MOST SECRET – KEEP OUT.

The hum and throb of powerful machinery could be heard coming up from the depths below, and the floor itself was vibrating all the time. The children could feel it through the soles of their shoes.

Miranda Piker now pushed forward and stood in front of Mr Wonka. She was a nasty-looking girl with a smug face and a smirk on her mouth, and whenever she spoke it was always with a voice that seemed to be saying, 'Everybody is a fool except me.'

'OK,' Miranda Piker said, smirking at Mr Wonka. 'So what's the big news? What's this stuff meant to do when you eat it?'

'Ah-ha,' said Mr Wonka, his eyes sparkling with glee. 'You'd never guess that, not in a million years. Now listen. All you have to do is sprinkle it over your cereal at breakfast-time, pretending it's sugar. Then you eat it. And then, exactly five seconds after that, you come out in bright red spots all over your face and neck.'

'What sort of a silly ass wants spots on his face at breakfast-time?' said Miranda Piker.

'Let me finish,' said Mr Wonka. 'So then your mother looks at you across the table and says, "My poor child. You must have chickenpox. You can't possibly go to school today." So you stay at home. But by lunch-time, the spots have all disappeared.'

'Terrific!' shouted Charlie. 'That's just what I want for the day we have exams!'

'That is the ideal time to use it,' said Mr Wonka. 'But you mustn't do it too often or it'll give the game away. Keep it for the really nasty days.'

'Father!' cried Miranda Piker. 'Did you hear what this stuff does? It's shocking! It mustn't be allowed!'

Mr Piker, Miranda's father, stepped forward

and faced Mr Wonka. He had a smooth white face like a boiled onion.

'Now see here, Wonka,' he said. 'I happen to be the headmaster of a large school, and I won't allow you to sell this rubbish to the children! It's . . . criminal! Why, you'll ruin the school system of the entire country!'

'I hope so,' said Mr Wonka.

'It's got to be stopped!' shouted Mr Piker, waving his cane.

'Who's going to stop it?' asked Mr Wonka. 'In my factory, I make things to please children. I don't care about grown-ups.'

'I am top of my form,' Miranda Piker said, smirking at Mr Wonka. 'And I've never missed a day's school in my life.'

'Then it's time you did,' Mr Wonka said.

'How dare you!' said Mr Piker.

'All holidays and vacations should be stopped!' cried Miranda. 'Children are meant to work, not play.'

'Quite right, my girl,' cried Mr Piker, patting Miranda on the top of the head. 'All work and no play has made you what you are today.'

'Isn't she wonderful?' said Mrs Piker, beaming at her daughter.

'Come on then, Father!' cried Miranda. 'Let's go down into the cellar and smash the machine that makes this dreadful stuff!'

'Forward!' shouted Mr Piker, brandishing his cane and making a dash for the little red door on which it said MOST SECRET – KEEP OUT.

'Stop!' said Mr Wonka. 'Don't go in there! It's terribly secret!'

'Let's see you stop us, you old goat!' shouted Miranda.

'We'll smash it to smithereens!' yelled Mr Piker. And a few seconds later the two of them had disappeared through the door.

There was a moment's silence.

Then, far off in the distance, from somewhere deep underground, there came a fearful scream.

'That's my husband!' cried Mrs Piker, going blue in the face.

There was another scream.

'And that's Miranda!' yelled Mrs Piker, beginning to hop around in circles. 'What's happening to them? What have you got down there, you dreadful beast?'

'Oh nothing much,' Mr Wonka answered. 'Just a lot of cogs and wheels and chains and things like that, all going round and round and round.'

'You villain!' she screamed. 'I know your tricks! You're grinding them into powder! In two minutes my darling Miranda will come pouring out of one of those dreadful pipes, and so will my husband!'

'Of course,' said Mr Wonka. 'That's part of the recipe.'

'It's what!'

'We've got to use one or two schoolmasters occasionally or it wouldn't work.'

'Did you hear him?' shrieked Mrs Piker, turning to the others. 'He admits it! He's nothing but a cold-blooded murderer!'

Mr Wonka smiled and patted Mrs Piker gently on the arm.

'Dear lady,' he said, 'I was only joking.'

'Then why did they scream?' snapped Mrs Piker. 'I distinctly heard them scream!'

'Those weren't screams,' Mr Wonka said. 'They were laughs.'

'My husband never laughs,' said Mrs Piker.

Mr Wonka flicked his fingers, and up came an Oompa Loompa.

'Kindly escort Mrs Piker to the boiler room,' Mr Wonka said. 'Don't fret, dear lady,' he went on, shaking Mrs Piker warmly by the hand. 'They'll all come out in the wash. There's nothing to worry about. Off you go. Thank you for coming. Farewell! Goodbye! A pleasure to meet you!'

'Listen, Charlie!' said Grandpa Joe. 'The Oompa-Loompas are starting to sing again!'

'Oh, Miranda Mary Piker!' sang the five Oompa-Loompas,

dancing about and laughing and beating madly on their
tiny drums.

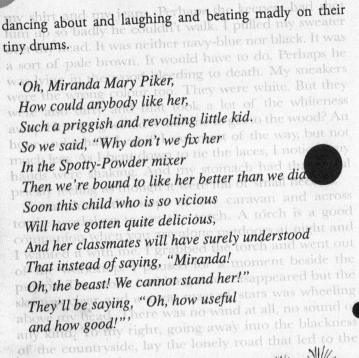

'Oh, Miranda Mary Piker,
How could anybody like her,
Such a priggish and revolting little kid.
So we said, "Why don't we fix her
In the Spotty-Powder mixer
Then we're bound to like her better than we did."
Soon this child who is so vicious
Will have gotten quite delicious,
And her classmates will have surely understood
That instead of saying, "Miranda!
Oh, the beast! We cannot stand her!"
They'll be saying, "Oh, how useful
and how good!"'

Beards and other disguises

Roald Dahl detested beards. He hated them. He absolutely couldn't stand them and never owned one himself. So when he invented the truly disgusting Mr Twit, he made sure that the first thing he gave him was a beard.

PASSPORT

Name: Mr Twit

Nationality: Hairy

Date of Birth: Mind your own business, you old hag!

Distinguishing marks: Very ugly

Roald Dahl's
thoughts on
HAIRY FACES

'As you know, an ordinary face like yours or mine simply gets a bit smudgy if it is not washed often enough, and there's nothing so awful about that. But a hairy face is a very different matter. Things cling to hairs, especially food. Things like gravy go right in among the hairs and stay there.'

Hairy
record breakers

The longest beard in the world belonged to Norwegian Hans Langseth. When he died in 1927, his record-breaking 5.33-metre-long beard was snipped off and taken to the Smithsonian Institution in Washington DC, USA.

According to *The Guinness Book of Records*, the world's longest ear hair belongs to Radhakant Bajpai from Naya Ganj, Uttar Pradesh in India. In 2003, it measured 13.2 cm long.

Xie Qiuping from Guangxi Province in China has the world's longest hair. In May 2004, it was measured for *The Guinness Book of Records* at an amazing 5.627 metres.

Cunning disguises

There is one thing that beards are good for – and that's disguising the person beneath. But if you don't have enough time to grow a beard before going under cover, here are more ideas for altering your appearance.

Dark sunglasses are a popular choice with celebrities who want to avoid the paparazzi. As well as hiding the eyes, they are very good at making the wearer look mysterious and terribly attractive.

A **fake moustache** will make you look very different.

Hats are always a good bet, especially if your hair is very easy to recognize. And if you have very big ears, go for one with flaps like Sherlock Holmes's deer stalker.

Stuck-on Rice Krispies make good warts! (But do not use glue. Try honey instead.)

Masters of disguise

Sherlock Holmes –

Sir Arthur Conan Doyle's fictional detective – often dressed up to stop others recognizing him. He starred in four novels and fifty-six short stories, in which he disguised himself as many characters, including a drunken bridegroom, a clergyman and a bookseller.

DETECTIVE INSPECTOR FRANCIS 'TANKY' SMITH was Leicester's very first private detective in Victorian times. He often dressed like the people he investigated. This way, he was able to overhear crooks and thieves talking about their plans, without making them suspicious. Carvings of his many disguises are displayed on the houses of Top Hat Terrace in the city.

Who's who?

If you were to spot someone wearing the following disguise, would you be able to guess who they actually were underneath . . .?

Gloves

This kind of person wears gloves all year round – even in summer and in the house. The only time they take them off is when they go to bed.

A first-class wig

This will be such an incredibly convincing wig that the only way to tell that it isn't real is if you give it a pull to see if it comes off.

Blue spit

This person will look as if they've been drinking blue ink. (Totally not recommended.) Their teeth might have a slight bluish tinge.

Slightly larger nostrils than ordinary people

Look closely. The rim of each nose-hole will be pink and curvy, like the rim of a certain kind of seashell.

Strange pupils

No, not the kind of children who enjoy homework or say that liver and onions is their favourite meal. These pupils are the tiny black dots in the middle of someone's eyes. In this kind of person, the dots keep changing colour . . .

(Clue: Look in Roald Dahl's most wicked book.)

Answer on page 144

Did you know?

Roald Dahl's *The Enormous Crocodile* is crammed with some of the most imaginative disguises ever. But how many people do they fool? Everyone? Or no one ...? If you're looking for the answer here, you're out of luck. You'll have to read the book to find out!

The very best
animal disguises

Swallowtail and pug moth caterpillars (and, once they turn into moths, their wings) have markings that look just like bird droppings. This is a brilliant way of staying safe from predators, who prefer tastier snacks.

Spider crabs stick live sea anemones and sponges to their shells. This helps them to look like the rest of the seabed.

The Arctic fox turns white in winter to match the snow.

A chameleon is a particularly clever type of lizard. Within minutes of arriving somewhere new, it can change colour to match its surroundings. Chameleons would make terrific spies.

What do you call a person with a beard, dark glasses, long raincoat and pink ear muffs?

Anything you like – he can't hear you.

Who works at MI5 on Christmas Day?

Mince spies!

Who was the first underwater spy?

James Pond.

Did you know?

Rumour has it that during the 1940s, Roald Dahl worked in Washington DC as a spy for the British intelligence service.

24

100% TRUE FACTS ABOUT REAL JAMES BONDS

 The UK's spies work for the Secret Intelligence Service (SIS).

 SIS (also known as MI6) collects secret intelligence overseas on behalf of the British government.

 MI stands for Military Intelligence.

MI5 protects the UK against threats to national security.

The head of SIS is known as 'C'. This is because the very first Chief of SIS – Captain Sir Mansfield Cumming RN – used to sign himself with just a 'C'. His successors all do the same.

 If you are interested in becoming a spy, visit: www.sis.gov.uk.

Mutt and Jeff

During the Second World War, two Norwegians, Helge Moe and Tor Glad, arrived on a Scottish beach in a rubber dinghy. At once, the two men turned themselves in to the police, claiming to be German spies. Later, they blew up a London flour store and an electricity generating station in Suffolk. But all was not as it seemed . . .

All along, the spies had been working for the British intelligence service, not the Germans. They were what is known as double agents - working for both sides but loyal only to one. Nicknamed Mutt and Jeff, they sent information to the enemy, leading them to believe that Britain was on the brink of invading Norway.

It was, of course, all lies.

Did you know?

Mutt and Jeff were American cartoon characters.

And the phrase 'Mutt 'n' Jeff' is Cockney rhyming slang for 'deaf'.

"Cockney rhyming slang"

How does it work? You take a pair of words that go together, like dog and bone, where the second word rhymes with the word you really want to say (phone). Then you use the first word of the pair, so 'phone' becomes 'dog'. Here are some classic cockney rhyming slang expressions:

Whistle
(whistle and flute) = suit

Mickey
(mickey mouse) = house

Apples
(apples and pears) = stairs

Butcher's
(butcher's hook) = look

Loaf
(loaf of bread) = head

China
(china plate) = mate

Porkies
(porky pies) = lies

Rosie
(Rosie Lee) = tea

It's not really clear why and where cockney rhyming slang originated. It's been around for a very long time. A favourite story is that it was developed by criminals so that they could talk without alerting the police to their plans.

DELTA ALPHA HOTEL LIMA

It might look like gobbledegook, but this is the way
a pilot or police officer would spell out Roald Dahl's
surname to avoid any misunderstandings of letters
which sound alike. Here are all the call signs,
just in case you want to spell something
super-clearly or make up your own
secret code . . .

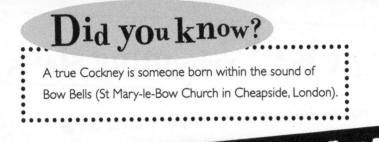

ALPHA
BRAVO
CHARLIE
DELTA
ECHO
FOXTROT
GOLF
HOTEL
INDIA

JULIET
KILO
LIMA
MIKE
NOVEMBER
OSCAR
PAPA
QUEBEC
ROMEO

SIERRA
TANGO
UNIFORM
VICTOR
WHISKY
X-RAY
ZULU

Champion code breakers

The Enigma machine was a coding device used by the Nazis during the Second World War. It looked like a typewriter but, when a letter was typed, a totally different letter would light up on the machine's display. This was the coded letter.

Inside Enigma, there was an impossibly complicated arrangement of wheels, plugs and reflectors that moved every time a letter was encoded. This meant that each time a letter was typed, it would be coded differently. DAHL might be coded as PLHU or AZWQ or even TWIT.

Teams of code breakers studied the seemingly indecipherable Enigma messages at Bletchley Park in Buckinghamshire. They had to crack the ever-changing Enigma codes over and over again, in order to decode top-secret enemy messages. Sometimes it could take up to ten months to break the code! But by 1943 they had the help of Colossus – a computer as big as a room.

How to make a coded message even more difficult to read

What you need:

Half a lemon	Paper
Small bowl	Iron
Fine paintbrush	Pillowcase

What you do:

1. **Squeeze** the lemon, catching the juice in a small bowl.
2. **Dip** the paintbrush into the lemon juice and use it to write a secret message on the paper. (Make sure to dip frequently, to stop the paintbrush drying out.)
3. **Wait** a few moments.
4. No, a little bit longer than that.
5. When the paper is **dry**, you can reveal your message. Place a pillowcase over the paper and run a warm iron over the pillowcase. Ask a grown-up first and always be very careful with irons — they can burn.
6. **Remove** the pillowcase and – ta daaaa! – the message will be revealed.

30

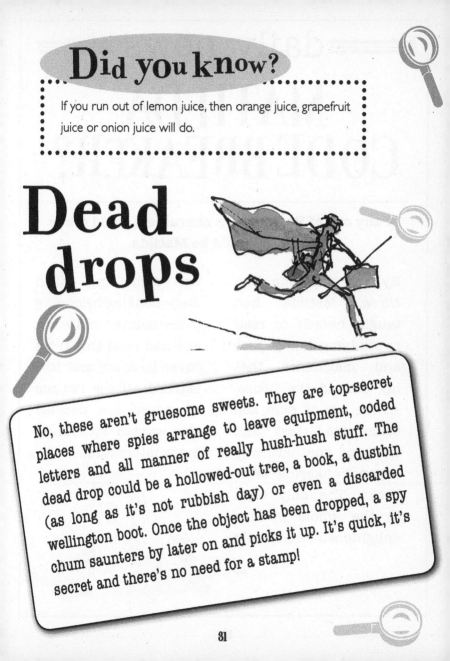

Dead drops

No, these aren't gruesome sweets. They are top-secret places where spies arrange to leave equipment, coded letters and all manner of really hush-hush stuff. The dead drop could be a hollowed-out tree, a book, a dustbin (as long as it's not rubbish day) or even a discarded wellington boot. Once the object has been dropped, a spy chum saunters by later on and picks it up. It's quick, it's secret and there's no need for a stamp!

MATILDA CODE BREAKER?

If any one of Roald Dahl's characters could crack codes, it would be Matilda.

By the time she was *three*, Matilda had taught herself to read by studying newspapers and magazines that lay around the house. At the age of *four*, she could read fast and well and she naturally began hankering after books. The only book in the whole of this enlightened household was something called *Easy Cooking* belonging to her mother, and when she had read this from cover to cover and had learned all the recipes by heart, she decided she wanted something more interesting.

The Baddies

Roald Dahl says...

'In every book or story there has to be somebody you can loathe. The fouler and more filthy a person is, the more fun it is to watch him getting scrunched.'

Imagine Roald Dahl's books without the baddies . . . *Matilda* just wouldn't be the same without Miss Trunchbull. The wicked aunts add pizazz to *James and the Giant Peach*. In *Danny the Champion of the World*, there's Mr Hazell. And in *Charlie and the Chocolate Factory*, the spoiled and filthy children are the bad guys.

Did you hear about the robbery last night?

Two clothes pegs held up a pair of pants.

tee hee!

Why did the robber have a bath before he held up the bank?

ho ho

He wanted to make a clean getaway.

Ha!

ho ho

Fictional baddies

In which books do these villains and villainesses appear?

- ☆ Bill Sikes
- ☆ Captain James Hook
- ☆ Cruella De Vil
- ☆ Farmer Boggis, Farmer Bunce and Farmer Bean
- ☆ Long John Silver

☆ Lord Voldermort

☆ Professor James Moriarty

☆ Sauron, the Dark Lord

☆ Shere Khan

☆ The White Witch

☆ The Wicked Witch of the West

Answers on page 144

☆ Harry Potter and the Philosopher's Stone by J. K. Rowling

☆ The Lion, the Witch and the Wardrobe by C. S. Lewis

☆ The Wonderful Wizard of Oz by L. Frank Baum

☆ The Hundred and One Dalmations by Dodie Smith

☆ Fantastic Mr Fox by Roald Dahl

☆ Treasure Island by Robert Louis Stevenson

☆ Peter Pan by J. M. Barrie

☆ Sherlock Holmes novels by Sir Arthur Conan Doyle

☆ Lord of the Rings by J. R. R. Tolkein

☆ The Jungle Book by Rudyard Kipling

☆ Oliver Twist by Charles Dickens

Real-life baddies

Captain Morgan

Sir Henry Morgan became famous for his exploits in the Caribbean during the seventeenth century. He carried out daring missions for the English governor of Jamaica, attacking the Spanish, then ransacking and destroying their ships. Even though his only pay was the booty that he won, he made a fortune. Despite the atrocities that he carried out, Morgan was knighted and made Lieutenant Governor of Jamaica. But eventually he lost the support of the British king, was sacked from his job and died in 1668 after years of ill health.

The Sea Queen of Connemara

Grace O'Malley was the daughter of an Irish chieftain. She was a fearless seafarer who captained a fleet of ships along Ireland's Atlantic coast, fighting her enemies and plundering their ships for treasure. Ruthless and tough, she made friends with Queen Elizabeth I when it suited her, sailing brazenly up the River Thames to meet the English queen and hobnob with Her Majesty.

Dick Turpin

Richard 'Dick' Turpin became famous for his dastardly exploits on the highways and byways of eighteenth-century England. After going on the run for cattle-stealing, he dabbled with burglary, before realizing that it was much easier to rob stagecoaches. So he became a highwayman, carrying out hundreds of robberies on the outskirts of London. It wasn't long before he added murder to his list of crimes. And when he stole a beautiful black mare named Black Bess, he became a horse thief too. Dick Turpin's short but varied and violent career ended in 1739, when he was hanged in York.

Blackbeard

He was perhaps the most famous pirate of them all. Called **Edward Teach**, he soon became known as **Blackbeard** – a much better name for a buccaneer. Blackbeard sailed the Caribbean Sea between 1716 and 1718, terrifying everyone he met and stealing huge amounts of valuables, food, drink and weapons from the ships that he raided.

He really did have a huge black beard. To make himself look extra scary, Blackbeard studded his hairy chin with lighted matches during battle. (Do NOT try this at home.) His brief reign of terror was ended in 1718 during a fierce sea battle. It is said to have taken five bullets and twenty stab wounds to finish him off. Then they chopped off his head to make really sure that he was dead.

One of Roald Dahl's baddies

The Pelican opened his gigantic beak and immediately the policemen pounced upon the burglar, who was crouching inside. They snatched his pistol away from him and dragged him out and put handcuffs on his wrists.

'Great Scott!' shouted the Chief of Police. 'It's the Cobra himself!'

'The who! The what!' everyone asked. 'Who's the Cobra?'

'The Cobra is the cleverest and most dangerous cat-burglar in the world!' said the Chief of Police.

From *The Giraffe and the Pelly and Me*

It's not just pirates who go to sea

Roald Dahl was a seasoned sailor. When he was young, he and his family chugged from Newcastle to Oslo in Norway every summer. And when they reached their final destination – a tiny island amongst the beautiful fjords – the Dahls scooted about in a battered old motorboat that they nicknamed the Hard Black Stinker. Whatever the weather, Roald's mother would take the helm, ferrying her family from one idyllic island to another.

Roald Dahl says...

'Nobody, not even the tiny children, bothered with lifebelts in those days. We would cling to the sides of our funny little white motorboat, driving through mountainous white-capped waves and getting drenched to the skin, while my mother calmly handled the tiller. There were times, I promise you, when the waves were so high that as we slid down into a trough the whole world disappeared from sight. Then up and up the little boat would climb, standing almost vertically on its tail, until we reached the crest of the next wave, and then it was like being on top of a foaming mountain.'

(You can read more about Roald Dahl's holidays in Norway in his book *Boy*.)

All at sea with Roald Dahl

'We're in the middle of the sea!'
cried James.

And indeed they were.
A strong current and a high
wind had carried the peach
so quickly away from the
shore that already the land
was out of sight. All around
them lay the vast black
ocean, deep and hungry.
Little waves were
bibbling against
the sides of the
peach.

From *James and
the Giant Peach*

43

What lies at the bottom of the sea and shakes?

A nervous wreck.

What did the sea say to the boat?

Nothing, it just waved.

Why did the intrepid explorer cross the ocean?

To get to the other tide.

Other Famous Voyagers

James Henry Trotter isn't the only one to sail off on a grand adventure, although he is probably the only explorer to use a giant peach.

Christopher Columbus (1451–1506)

Columbus is famous for discovering the Americas. He went backwards and forwards between Spain and the New World, but he never actually set foot in North America.

Captain James Cook (1728–79)

A British explorer and map maker, Cook clocked up an astonishing number of seafaring 'firsts'. He made the first European contact with the east coast of Australia, he was the first European to discover the Hawaiian Islands and he made the first maps of Newfoundland and New Zealand. As if that wasn't enough, he made the first recorded round-the-world trip too. It didn't stop him being eaten by cannibals though!

Charles Darwin (1809–82)

This British naturalist showed how species develop, or evolve, over time. During his five-year voyage on the HMS *Beagle*, he famously visited the Galapagos Islands off South America where he found that species of animals varied from those on the mainland. When he returned home, he wrote the bestselling *On the Origin of Species*.

Thor Heyerdahl (1914–2002)

This intrepid Norwegian explorer and writer wanted to show that people from South America could have travelled to Polynesia in the South Pacific and settled there long ago. In 1947, using balsa wood and old-fashioned methods, he built a raft called *Kon-Tiki* and sailed her nearly 7,000 km from Peru to the Taumotu Islands in French Polynesia – just to prove a point!

Bad ends

Highwaymen and gibbets

Most highwaymen were hanged and then their bodies were hung from gibbets at a crossroads. A gibbet was like a signpost with only one arm. Often their bodies were suspended from the gibbet in an iron cage and left there to rot. This was not only to warn other wrongdoers, but to stop their ghosts from causing mischief elsewhere – people believed crossroads would confuse ghosts, leaving them unable to decide which road to take.

Pirates and Execution Dock

For over 400 years, captured pirates were brought to London to be executed. They were hanged on a special gallows near the Thames, so that when the tide came in it would wash over the body. The custom was to let three tides wash over the body before it was taken away. More notorious pirates were then covered with tar (to preserve them) and hung on a gibbet or in irons along the Thames at Graves Point to warn sailors of the price of mutiny and piracy.

The most famous pirate to be executed here was Captain William Kidd on 23 May 1701. Execution Dock's last victims were executed for murder and mutiny in 1830.

4

Disastrous Disasters

Roald Dahl's books are peppered with terrible disasters and unbelievably hideous happenings. James Henry Trotter's relatives have a particularly dreadful time. His parents are eaten by an enormous angry rhinoceros, which has escaped from London Zoo. And his aunts meet a very nasty end.

Roald Dahl says...

'When you're writing a book, with people in it as opposed to animals, it is no good having people who are ordinary, because they are not going to interest your readers at all. Every writer in the world has to use the characters that have something interesting about them and this is even more true in children's books. I find that the only way to make my characters really interesting to children is to exaggerate all their good or bad qualities, and so if a person is nasty or bad or cruel, you make them very nasty, very bad, very cruel. If they are ugly, you make them extremely ugly. That, I think, is fun and makes an impact.'

The world's worst volcanic eruptions

Where?	When?	How many died?
Krakatoa, Indonesia	1883	36,000
Mount Pelée, Martinique, West Indies	1902	Over 30,000
Mount Vesuvius, Italy	79	20,000
Mount Etna, Sicily	1669	20,000
Tambora, Java	1815	10–12,000
Mount Skaptar, Iceland	1783	10,000
Mount Kelud, Indonesia	1919	5,000
Mount Vesuvius, Italy	1631	4,000
Galunggung, Java	1822	4,000
Mount Lamington, New Guinea	1951	3–5,000

Disastrous facts

- On average, a minor earthquake strikes the British Isles every four days.

- About twenty per cent of the world's population lives under the threat of a volcano. (That's over one billion people!)

- Tsunami waves, which can be caused by undersea earthquakes and volcanic eruptions, travel across oceans at speeds of up to 1,000 km per hour. That's nearly three times the speed of a Formula One car.

- You're twice as likely to see a tornado in the UK than you are in the USA.

What to do in an earthquake

1. If you are indoors, duck under a sturdy desk or table and stay there until the ground stops shaking.
2. If you are in a shop, move away from display shelves.
3. If you are outside, go to a big open space.

4. If you are near buildings, shelter in a doorway.
5. If you are in a wheelchair, move to cover, lock your wheels and protect your head with your arms.
6. If you are on a mountain, watch out for rock slides.
7. If you are at the beach, move to higher ground or inland.

8. If you are at a football match, stay in your seat and protect your head with your arms.
9. If you are in a car or bus, get the driver to pull over. Steer clear of bridges.
10. After an earthquake, be prepared for aftershocks. You might need to take cover again.

How can you tell when a volcano is angry?

It blows its top.

What did the ground say to the earthquake?

You crack me up!

Ha! Ha! Ha! Ha! Ha! Ha! Ha! Ha! Ha!

I am crying with laughter!

Bad weather

Roald Dahl thought that the best place to spend January was in a hot bath. He wasn't too keen on February either, calling it the 'fiercest and bitterest month of all'.

Extreme weather — what is it?

BLIZZARD	a severe snowstorm with high winds
HEATWAVE	a long period of abnormally hot weather
HURRICANE	a tropical spinning storm with wind speeds of over 118 km an hour. Hurricanes are also known as typhoons or cyclones, depending on where in the world you are.
MONSOON	alternate very wet and very dry seasons
TORNADO	a moving funnel of violently spinning winds
TROPICAL STORM	a storm with winds ranging from approximately 48 to 118 km an hour

Naming hurricanes and tropical storms

The National Hurricane Center of the USA has named Atlantic hurricanes and tropical storms since 1953. Since 1979, six lists of alternating women's and men's names have been used in rotation. But if ever there's

2007/2013	2008/2014	2009/2015
Andrea	Arthur	Ana
Barry	Bertha	Bill
Chantal	Cristobal	Claudette
Dean	Dolly	Danny
Erin	Edouard	Erika
Felix	Fay	Fred
Gabrielle	Gustav	Grace
Humberto	Hanna	Henri
Ingrid	Ike	Ida
Jerry	Josephine	Joaquin
Karen	Kyle	Kate
Lorenzo	Laura	Larry
Melissa	Marco	Mindy
Noel	Nana	Nicholas
Olga	Omar	Odette
Pablo	Paloma	Peter
Rebekah	Rene	Rose
Sebastien	Sally	Sam
Tanya	Teddy	Teresa
Van	Vicky	Victor
Wendy	Wilfred	Wanda

a really destructive hurricane, its name is removed. For example, there will never be another Hurricane Katrina after the 2005 hurricane of that name devastated New Orleans, USA.

If you fancy keeping an eye on hurricanes, here are six handy lists. And for more hurricane names from around the world, check out: www.nhc.noaa.gov/aboutnames.shtml

2010/2016

Alex
Bonnie
Colin
Danielle
Earl
Fiona
Gaston
Hermine
Igor
Julia
Karl
Lisa
Matthew
Nicole
Otto
Paula
Richard
Shary
Tomas
Virginie
Walter

2011/2017

Arlene
Bret
Cindy
Don
Emily
Franklin
Gert
Harvey
Irene
Jose
Katia
Lee
Maria
Nate
Ophelia
Philippe
Rina
Sean
Tammy
Vince
Whitney

2012/2018

Alberto
Beryl
Chris
Debby
Ernesto
Florence
Gordon
Helene
Isaac
Joyce
Kirk
Leslie
Michael
Nadine
Oscar
Patty
Rafael
Sandy
Tony
Valerie
William

The Beaufort scale

In 1805, **Sir Francis Beaufort** invented a way of measuring the wind speed at sea. Each wind speed was given a number and a description. It was so useful that the Beaufort scale was later adapted to work on land too. Wind speeds rated twelve are rarely found outside tropical revolving storms.

NUMBER	WIND SPEED	DESCRIPTION	SEA CONDITIONS	LAND CONDITIONS
0	0 km per sec	Calm	Sea like a mirror	Smoke rises vertically
1	1–6	Light air	Ripples	Smoke drifts
2	7–11	Light breeze	Small wavelets	Leaves rustle
3	12–19	Gentle breeze	Large wavelets	Small twigs move
4	20–29	Moderate breeze	Whitecaps	Small branches move
5	30–39	Fresh breeze	Many whitecaps in long form	Small trees sway
6	40–50	Strong breeze	Larger waves and spray	Large branches move
7	51–62	Moderate gale	Foam from waves	Whole trees in motion
8	63–75	Fresh gale	Waves crests break	Twigs break off trees
9	76–87	Strong gale	High waves	Chimney pots and slates removed
10	88–102	Whole gale	Very high waves	Trees uprooted
11	103–117	Storm	Exceptionally high waves	Widespread damage
12	More than 117	Hurricane	Air filled with foam	Considerable and widespread damage to structures

Deadliest plagues

A plague is an infectious disease that spreads easily and quickly. Without treatment, it can be fatal. Plagues have killed millions of people throughout history. Here are two of the worst outbreaks to hit the UK.

The Black Death

WHERE: From Asia to Europe

WHEN: 1348

WHAT HAPPENED: Swellings appeared in the groin or armpits before spreading all over the body. Next came black or purple spots. Finally, there was a gush of blood from the nose.

HOW MANY DEATHS: At least 75 million people died.

The Great Plague of London

WHERE: London and other parts of the UK

WHEN: 1665-66

WHAT HAPPENED: Chills, fever, headaches and swellings

HOW MANY DEATHS: Between 75,000 and 100,000 people died - up to twenty per cent of London's population.

The Great Plague of London was eventually wiped out by another disaster – the Great Fire of London. The plague was carried by infected fleas who lived on rats. When the terrible fire killed the rats, the plague died with them.

The worst plague in history

Known as Spanish flu, the influenza that swept round the world in 1918–19 was a global disaster. Up to 50 million people died in a single year – more than had died in the four years of the First World War. A fifth of the world's population was affected and, unusually, the flu was most deadly for people between the ages of twenty to forty.

5

POiSon

WARNING TO READERS:
Do not try to make
George's Marvellous Medicine
yourselves at home.
It could be dangerous.

George's Marvellous Quiz

Study the following ingredients carefully. Which of them would you NOT find in George's Marvellous Medicine? (Clue: there are five real ingredients and five fake ones.)

- FLEA POWDER FOR DOGS
- CAT OINTMENT FOR CATS WITH MANGE, NITS, FLEAS AND VERY BAD TEMPERS
- DARK BROWN GLOSS PAINT
- ENGINE OIL
- A TIN OF CABBAGE SOUP
- CASTOR OIL
- THE MOULD FROM A THREE-WEEK-OLD CHEESE SANDWICH
- A BOTTLE OF 'EXTRA-HOT' CHILLI SAUCE
- A BRUSSELS SPROUTS SMOOTHIE
- PIG PILLS FOR PIGS WITH PORK PRICKLES, TENDER TROTTERS, BRISTLE BLIGHT AND SWINE SICKNESS

Answers on page 144

Poisonous Plants

Buttercups (*Ranunculus species*)	poisonous sap can seriously injure the digestive system
Daffodil (*Narcissus*)	bulbs are poisonous
Drooping laurel (*Leucothoe davisiae*)	all parts are poisonous; can be fatal
Laburnum	all parts are poisonous
Mistletoe (*Viscum album*)	poisonous berries
Monkshood (*Acontium*)	all parts are poisonous
Rosary pea (*Abrus precatorius*)	a single seed can cause death
Water hemlock (*Cicut species*)	all parts are fatal

A Roald Dahl story
not seen for thirty years!

Roald Dahl once thought of an ingenious way of catching mice without poisoning them. He wrote a short story, based on his idea, which appeared in the first Puffin Annual in 1974 and hasn't been printed in full since.

So, if you're ever overrun by the little blighters, read this to find out how to deal with them.

The Upside-down Mice

Once upon a time there lived an old man of eighty-seven whose name was Labon. All his life he had been a quiet and peaceful person. He was very poor and very happy.

When Labon discovered that he had mice in his house, he did not at first bother himself greatly about it. But the mice multiplied. They kept right on multiplying and finally there came a time when he could stand it no longer.

'This is too much,' he said. 'This really is going a bit too far.'

He hobbled out of the house and down the road to a shop where he bought himself some mousetraps, a piece of cheese and some glue.

When he got home, he put the glue on the underneath of the mousetraps and stuck them to the ceiling. Then he baited them carefully with pieces of cheese and set them to go off.

That night when the mice came out of their holes and saw the mousetraps on the ceiling, they thought it a tremendous joke. They walked around on the floor, nudging each other and pointing up with their front paws and roaring with laughter. After all it was pretty silly, mousetraps on the ceiling.

When Labon came down the next morning and saw that there were no mice caught in the traps, he smiled but said nothing.

He took a chair and put glue on the bottom of its legs and stuck it upside down to the ceiling, near the mousetraps. He did the same with the table, the television set and the lamp. He took everything that was on the floor and stuck it upside down on the ceiling. He even put a little carpet up there.

The next night when the mice came out of their holes they were still joking and laughing about what they had seen the night before. But now, when they looked up at the ceiling, they stopped laughing very suddenly.

'Good gracious me!' cried one. 'Look up there! There's the floor!'

'Heavens above!' shouted another. 'We must be standing on the ceiling.'

'I'm beginning to feel a little giddy,' said another.

'All the blood's going to my head,' said another.

'This is terrible!' said a very senior mouse with long whiskers. 'This is really terrible! We must do something about it at once.'

'I shall faint if I have to stand on my head any longer!' shouted a young mouse.

'Me too!'

'I can't stand it!'

'Save us! Do something, somebody, quick!'

'I know what we'll do,' said the very senior mouse. 'We'll all stand on our heads, then anyway we'll be the right way up.'

Obediently, they all stood on their heads, and after a long time, one by one, they fainted from a rush of blood to their brains.

When Labon came down the next morning, the floor was littered with mice. Quickly, he gathered them up and popped them all in a basket.

So the thing to remember is this: WHENEVER THE WORLD SEEMS TO BE TERRIBLY UPSIDE DOWN, MAKE SURE YOU KEEP YOUR FEET FIRMLY ON THE GROUND.

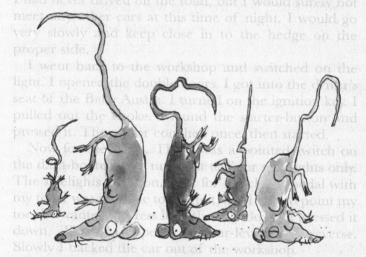

Topsy-turvy quiz question

Can you think of another Roald Dahl book in which two very objectionable characters find that their world has turned upside down?

Answer on page 144

What **R**O**a**ld **Dahl** thought about Snakes

When Roald was twenty, he was working for the Shell Oil Company. They sent him to East Africa, and he loved everything about it – except the snakes: 'Oh, those snakes! How I hated them! They were the only fearful thing about Tanganyika, and a newcomer very quickly learned to identify most of them and to know which were deadly and which were simply poisonous. The killers, apart from the black mambas, were the green mambas, the cobras and the tiny little puff adders that looked very much like small sticks lying motionless in the middle of a dusty path, and so easy to step on.'

(You can read more about Roald Dahl's first job in Africa in his book *Going Solo*.)

Deadly snake facts

The black mamba is the largest venomous snake in Africa and the second largest in the world. It's the fastest snake in the world and also the most aggressive. It's quite long too, with an average length of 2.5 metres and a maximum length of 4.5 metres. The black mamba actually gets its name from the colour of the inside of its mouth – its skin is greyish-olive. Its bite is often fatal. Roald Dahl said it was the only snake that had no fear of man and would deliberately attack people on sight. No wonder he was scared of it.

The green mamba is smaller than the black mamba, but just as poisonous. Luckily, it is not so aggressive, so you're less likely to be bitten by it. The green mamba is a pretty snake – it has a brilliant green skin with a lighter green underside.

The cobra kills its prey, usually small rodents or birds, by injecting poison through its almost-hollow fangs. It can be recognized by its hood – a flap of skin and muscle behind the head. This hood flares outwards, making it look even scarier than before. Cobras can be black, brown, yellowy-white or colours in between. In humans, only one in ten bites is fatal. But you'd be best advised to get every bite checked out.

Strangely, the **puff adder** is actually a type of viper. It gets its name from the way it puffs up and deflates, while hissing loudly, to threaten enemies. The smallest snake grows to a maximum of twenty-eight centimetres – shorter than a ruler. But even though it's small, it is still poisonous.

British Snake facts

There are three species of snake found in Britain. None of them presents a serious danger, and killing any reptile in the UK is now a criminal offence.

The **grass**, or **ringed**, **snake** is the largest British snake and can reach up to 120 cm in length. It is a slender snake, green, olive or brown in colour, with a distinct black-edged yellow or white crescent on each side of its neck. It lives mainly on frogs and is a strong swimmer. It is the only egg-laying snake in Britain and can lay as many as forty leathery-skinned eggs at a time. The eggs take around ten weeks to hatch. The grass snake is not poisonous. To defend itself it makes a very bad smell! Or it will go limp and pretend to be dead.

The **smooth snake** is a very rare species, found only in Dorset, Hampshire and Surrey. It grows to around sixty centimetres in length and is grey or brown in colour with two rows of dark spots along its back and spots along its sides. On the top of its head is a dark figure of eight marking. It lives mainly on other reptiles, but may also eat small mammals. It is not poisonous and kills its prey by constriction or squeezing. The smooth snake gives birth to live young, from five to fifteen at a time, depending on the size of the mother.

The **adder** is the only venomous British snake – but its bite is unlikely to kill. However, adders should NOT be handled and you should seek medical attention if you are bitten. Adders are small snakes, usually up to sixty centimetres in length, but they're not as slender as grass or smooth snakes. Males tend to be dirty yellow or white in colour; females are much more brown or reddish. Both sexes have a dark zigzag stripe along the back and dark bars or blotches along the sides. There is an X-shaped or V-shaped mark on top of the head.

Adders eat small mammals and other reptiles, using their venom to kill them. Once bitten, the prey animal will usually die in a few minutes and the adder will use its keen sense of smell to track it. Adders give birth to around five to fifteen live young, who are much redder than their parents. Adders are widespread over the whole of mainland Britain, on Anglesey and the Isle of Wight, particularly in heathland and moorland.

What to do if you are
bitten by an adder

- DO NOT attempt to capture or kill the snake.

- Keep calm and keep the bitten area as still as possible. You could put on a sling or a bandage, but not a tourniquet.

- Seek medical attention.

- DO NOT attempt any other treatment like trying to suck out the venom.

Did you know?

There are no snakes in Ireland. There is a legend that St Patrick drove them all into the sea, banishing them for eternity. But the truth is that snakes are cold-blooded animals and so can't survive in places where the ground is frozen all year round. Ireland only thawed out from the last ice age 15,000 years ago, and since then it's been surrounded by water. So no snakes have been able to get there.

6

Parties!

Roald Dahl adored fabulous
food – he was fond of cooking
it too. And he liked nothing
more than gathering family
and friends round a table
for a delicious meal, before
producing his famous red
plastic box and inviting
everyone to help themselves
to his favourite chocolates.
Mmm . . .

Roald Dahl's top ❸ tasty teatime treats

❶ Hot-house eggs

A delicious combination of fried bread and fried egg. Cut a circle out of a slice of bread. Fry the bread on both sides. Break an egg into the hole. Sizzle until the egg is cooked. Mmm . . .

❷ Creamy KitKat pudding

Put a layer of KitKats in the bottom of a dish. Then a layer of whipped cream. Then a layer of KitKats. Then another of whipped cream and so on for as long as you like. Put the whole thing in the freezer. Serve in slices when frozen.

🍴③ Crunchy jelly

Follow the instructions to make a jelly. Then, just before it has set, stir in a handful of hundreds and thousands. Pop it in the fridge and then wait until it has set properly to enjoy this wibbly-crunchy treat.

Unusual food from around the world

Deep-fried dragonflies (Bali)
Chocolate-covered ants (Japan)
Sheep's head (Norway)
Fried monkey toes (Thailand)
Roasted camel (the Middle East)
Freeze-dried food (in space)

Did you know?

When you eat a meal, you can swallow up to a litre of air. That might cause an awful lot of whizzpopping!

From yuck to mmm . . .

As you get older, some of your taste buds die. As a baby, you have around 10,000 taste buds, but by the time you're old only about 5,000 remain. This is why certain foods that taste horribly strong when you are young can become more appealing as you get older. But the fact remains that some people will never like Brussels sprouts.

What the stars like to eat

Jennifer Aniston – tortilla crisps
George Clooney – steak
Tom Cruise – Italian food
Angelina Jolie – burger and fries
Britney Spears – chicken and dumplings

Fictional food

Roald Dahl's characters are treated to a dazzling array of culinary delights. But do you know which books these meals come from?

Tender juicy lettuce leaves

Snozzcumbers and frobscottle

Squiggly spaghetti

Chicken, turkey, goose and duck

Swudge — edible grass made of soft, minty sugar

Answers on page 145

Cadbury's Dairy Milk

When **Roald Dahl** started his first job, he bought himself a bar of Cadbury's Dairy Milk chocolate every lunch-time . . .

'By the time I got back to the office I had eaten all the chocolate, but I never threw away the silver paper. On my very first day I rolled it into a tiny ball and left it on my desk. On the second day I rolled the second bit of silver paper around the first bit. And every day from then on I added another bit of silver paper to that little ball. The ball began to grow. In one year it had become very nearly as big as a tennis ball and just as round. It was extraordinarily heavy . . . I never lost my chocolate silver-paper ball and today it sits, as it has done ever since I started to write, on the old pine table beside my writing chair.'

The silver ball is still on the table in Roald Dahl's writing hut.

Likes and dislikes

Roald Dahl liked other things besides chocolate.
Take this quick quiz to see how much you know about the things he liked and the things he didn't.

1. Was his favourite colour • • •

a) pink,
b) sage green or
c) yellow?

2. What was Roald Dahl's least favourite celebration?

a) His birthday.
b) Christmas.
c) Halloween.

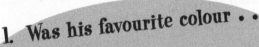

3. What did he like to eat the most?

a) Sushi.

b) Caviar.

c) Squidgy chocolate cake.

4. What was Roald Dahl's favourite pastime?

a) Mushroom-picking.

b) Litter-picking.

c) Nose-picking.

5. What was Roald Dahl's favourite sound?

a) The whirring of an electric lawnmower.

b) Buzzing bumblebees.

c) Piano music.

Answers on page 145.

Dahl-tastic
party games

Why not hold a party with a Dahl twist? Here are some top ideas for games . . .

Pin the ears on the BFG

Draw a large picture of the BFG without ears and pin it on a door. Make two enormous flappy ears from card and attach a drawing pin to each one. Make sure they don't fall out! (If you have a couple of pink balloons spare, use these instead. But don't blow them up first!) Each guest is blindfolded, in turn, and has to pin the ears on to the right parts of the picture. The pinholes are initialled and the guest with the best attempt wins.

Gruesome twosomes

Make a list of characters from one of Roald Dahl's books to equal half the number of guests. For example, if you have twenty guests, you will need ten names. Write the name of each character on two cards. As the guests arrive, give each one a card. They must go around the room pretending to be their character until they find their partner.

The more outrageous the character, the more fun you'll have. *Charlie and the Chocolate Factory* is bursting with them. Try Augustus Gloop, Veruca Salt, Mike Teavee, Violet Beauregarde, an Oompa-Loompa, Willy Wonka . . .

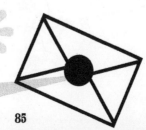

The whipple-scrumptious chocolate game

You will need: a wrapped chocolate bar, a knife and fork, various bits of clothing (hat, gloves and scarf at least – particularly the gloves!) and a die.

Put everything on a table and ask the players to sit round the table in a circle. Take turns at rolling the die. The first person to roll a six has to put on the clothes and try to unwrap and eat the chocolate, using the knife and fork. They have to keep going until the next six is thrown and then that player takes over, putting on the clothes and carrying on where the first player left off. The winner is the first person to finish the chocolate.

Willy Wonka says

Ask your party guests to line up in front of you. Tell them that they must obey you if your instruction starts with the words 'Willy Wonka says'. Now begin by saying something like, 'Willy Wonka says, put your hands on your head.' Check that everyone has done this. Follow with more and more instructions, such as, 'Willy Wonka says, wiggle your foot in the air,' then 'Willy Wonka says, shout Happy Birthday!' If anyone gets it wrong, they're out. You can try to trick the players too, by giving instructions without the magic words, such as simply, 'Stick your finger in your ear.' Anyone that follows this instruction is out because you didn't say 'Willy Wonka says'! The winner is the last person remaining.

Counting rhymes

What do you do when you need to choose someone to be 'it'? Easy, use one of these handy rhymes. Point to a different person on each beat of the rhymes.

1

Eeny, meeny, miny, moe,
Catch a baby by the toe.
If it squeals let it go,
Eeny, meeny, miny, moe.

2

3

Ip dip do,
The cat's got the flu,
The monkey's got the chickenpox,
So out goes you!

4

Counting sheep

Shepherds count their sheep a lot. This isn't because they have trouble sleeping, but because they have to keep a close eye on their flocks. Long ago, shepherds in northern England and southern Scotland had a special way of counting sheep. But they didn't stick to one, two, three ... They used words that came from old Celtic languages – and every region had a different set of words. Here's just one of them:

1. Yan
2. Tan
3. Tethera
4. Pethera
5. Pimp
6. Sethera
7. Methera
8. Hovera
9. Covera
10. Dik

Later, the words were used in playground rhymes.

Yan, tan, tethera, tethera, pethera, pimp.
Yon owd yowe's far-welted, and this yowe's got a limp
Sethera, methera, hovera, and covera up to dik.
Aye, we can deal wi' 'em all, and wheer's me crook and stick?

How to make a
Dahl-themed
fortune counter

You will need:
A square piece of paper, about twenty centimetres by twenty centimetres
A pen
Some fingers

Before you start:
Remember to press firmly whenever you fold the paper.

What you do:

1. Fold the paper from corner to corner. Unfold. Now fold it from the other corner to corner. Unfold again.
2. The centre of the paper is where the fold marks cross.
3. Take each corner of the paper and fold it to the centre, so all the points meet.
4. Turn the paper over.
5. Again, fold all four corners to the centre.
6. Number each triangle from one to eight.
7. Now fold each triangle back and write a Dahlesque task on each one. (See next page for ideas.)
8. Fold the numbered triangles back into place, flip the counter and slide your forefingers and thumbs under the four flaps.

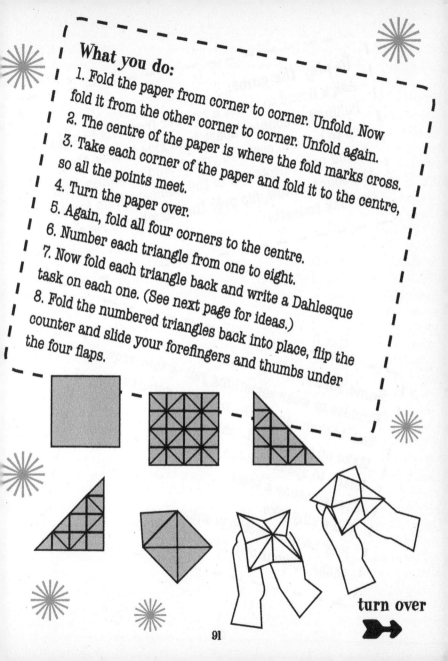

turn over ▶▶

To play the game:

Ask a friend to select a number from one to eight. Pulling the counter apart from side to side, then top to bottom, count to your friend's number. Your friend now selects one of the numbers from inside the counter. Now, flip over that number to reveal the task beneath!

Some ideas:

Promise to wear something yellow tomorrow.

Talk backwards for the next ten minutes.

Make up an Oompa-Loompa dance.

Learn to speak like the BFG.

Give someone a treat.

Tell a silly joke.

Play an unexpected prank.

Make up your own revolting rhyme.

Silly
(and not so silly)
scribbles

Roald Dahl always used a
pencil to write his books,
never a pen and never ever a
computer. At the beginning
of each writing session,
he would have six sharpened
pencils. By the end, he
would have six
blunt pencils
and a pile of
yellow paper,
covered in
his spidery
handwriting.

ESIO TROT, ESIO TROT,
TEG REGGIB REGGIB!
EMOC NO, ESIO TROT,
WORG PU, FFUP PU, TOOHS PU!
GNIRPS PU, WOLB PU, LLEWS PU!
EGROG! ELZZUG! FFUTS! PLUG!
TUP NO TAF, ESIO TROT, TUP NO TAF!
TEG NO, TEG NO! ELBBOG DOOF!

From *Esio Trot*

Did you know?

Famous painter, engineer and sculptor Leonardo da Vinci (1452–1519) was very good at mirror writing. He filled page after page with silly-looking scribbles that could be read when the paper was reflected in a mirror. He even made scientific notes and labelling diagrams in this way. But why did he bother? Was it because he was left-handed? (It's much easier for left-handed people to write in this way.) Or was it because he wanted to keep his ideas secret? No one really knows …

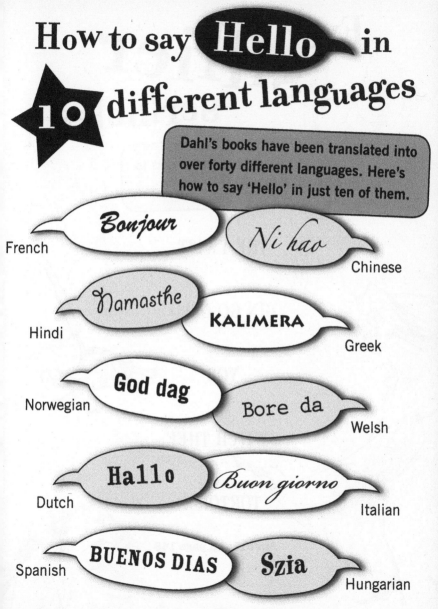

Even sillier scribbles

Can you unscramble these odd phrases to find the titles of Roald Dahl's books?

THE TWIST

GIN GO OSLO

YOB

SWITCH THEE

TORTOISE

Answers on page 145

96

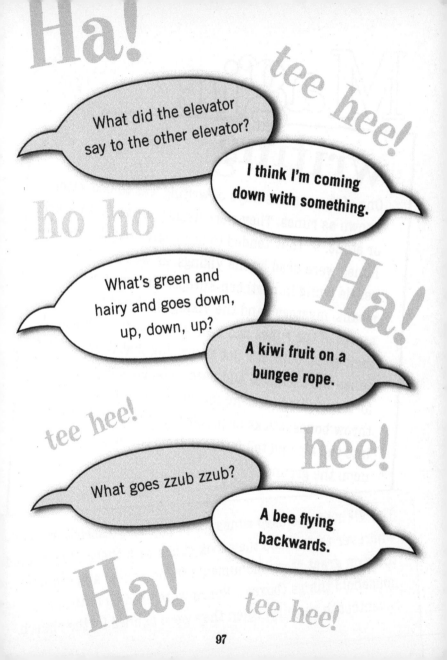

Magic writing

One of the earliest ways of writing was to use letters known as runes. They were usually carved into wood or stone, so they tended to be mostly straight lines. Runes were used by the Vikings, as well as other people living in northern Europe. The word 'rune' means 'mystery', and the Vikings believed that the secret of the runes had been given to them by one of their gods, Odin. It's not surprising that they thought runes were magical and used them for spells and fortune telling (casting the runes) – when they would throw bones, sticks or pebbles engraved with runes into the air and tell fortunes from the way they fell upon the ground.

The Vikings also used runes for poetry and inscriptions, and wherever they sailed they took runes with them. They carved them on great stone monuments (runestones) and ordinary household things (boxes). Runes were used up until the seventeenth century, when they were banned by the church.

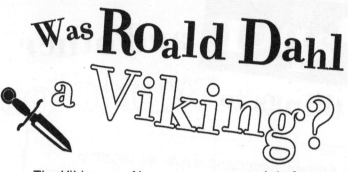

Was Roald Dahl a Viking?

The Vikings, or Norsemen, came mainly from Norway and Denmark – and both Roald's parents came from Norway. So, though he was born in Wales and lived most of his life in the UK, you might also say he was a Viking!

An alphabet of runes

a b c d e f g h i j k l

m n o p r s t u w x y

(There were no runes for 'q', 'v' or 'z'.)

Paper and other things to write on

The Ancient Egyptians wrote on papyrus (which is where the word 'paper' comes from). It was made from beaten strips of papyrus plants that grew along the edges of the river Nile. Papyrus paper was being made at least 5,000 years ago.

If you didn't live in a country hot enough to grow papyrus, then you could use parchment (made of processed sheepskin) or vellum (processed calfskin). In China, documents were originally written on bone or bamboo (bit heavy and awkward) or silk (very expensive).

All these early writing materials were very rare and costly.

True paper, using wood pulp, was invented in China, about 2,000 years ago, but it wasn't until the twelfth century that paper-making came to Europe.

Roald Dahl Says...

'To me, the most important and difficult thing about writing fiction is to find the plot. Good original plots are very hard to come by. You never know when a lovely idea is going to flit suddenly into your mind but, by golly, when it does come along, you grab it with both hands and hang on to it tight. The trick is to write it down at once, otherwise you'll forget it.

'I have had this book ever since I started trying to write seriously. There are ninety-eight pages in the book. I've counted them. And just about every one of those pages is filled up on both sides with these so-called story ideas. Many are no good. But just about every story and every children's book I have ever written has started out as a three- or four-line note in this little, much-worn red-covered volume.'

10 ways to be a brilliant children's author

(like Roald Dahl)

1. Think up a strong plot that will gather momentum all the way to the end of the book.

2. Make your reader laugh (actual loud belly laughs) . . .

3. . . . and squirm . . .

4. . . . and become enthralled . . .

5. . . . and tense . . .

6. . . . and excited.

7. (If your reader is shouting, 'Don't stop!' you've done a good job.)

8. Add an element of farce – the sillier the better.

9. Add a character that the reader can loathe.

10. Begin to write. Everything starts to develop once you put pencil to paper.

How to address a letter to someone very important

	On the envelope	At the top of the letter
A KING	HM the King	Your Majesty
A QUEEN	HM the Queen	Your Majesty
THE PRINCE OF WALES	HRH the Prince of Wales	Your Royal Highness
A PRINCESS	HRH the Princess A	Your Royal Highness
A DUKE	His Grace the Duke of B	My Lord Duke or Dear Duke of B
A DUCHESS	Her Grace the Duchess of C	Madam or Dear Duchess of C
AN EARL	The Rt Hon the Earl of D	My Lord or Dear Lord D
A COUNTESS	The Rt Hon the Countess of E	Madam or Dear Lady E

Roald Dahl's lucky break

After returning from the Second World War, Roald Dahl met up with C. S. Forester, a famous British novelist. It was Forester's job to interview Roald about his adventures as a fighter pilot. But Roald was terrible at telling stories aloud, so he offered instead to write down what had happened. The story was called 'A Piece of Cake' and this is C. S. Forester's reply.

Dear RD,

You were meant to give me notes, not a finished story. I'm bowled over. Your piece is marvellous. It is the work of a gifted writer. I didn't touch a word of it. I sent it at once under your name to my agent, Harold Matson, asking him to offer it to the *Saturday Evening Post* with my personal recommendation. You will be happy to hear that the *Post* accepted it immediately and have paid one thousand dollars. Mr Matson's commission is ten per cent. I enclose his cheque for nine hundred dollars. It's all yours. As you will see from Mr Matson's letter, which I also enclose, the *Post* is asking if you will write more stories for them. I do hope you will. Did you know you were a writer? With my very best wishes and congratulations,

CS Forester.

Roald Dahl says...

'At the age of eight I became a mad diary enthusiast . . . I was a bit of a loner in those days and a bit of a dreamer and some of the things I wrote down for the next five or six years were thoughts that I don't think I would have dared even to speak out aloud to myself. That's the beauty of writing. You find that you can actually write things down that are quite outlandish and outrageous and you feel all the better for it.'

Famous
diary writers

Samuel Pepys (1633–1703) told what it was like to live through the Great Plague of London and the Great Fire of London.

Captain James Cook (1728–79) kept a diary of the 'remarkable occurrences' that took place during his historic voyage to New Zealand, Tasmania and Australia.

Anne Frank (1929–45) was a young Jewish girl who lived in Amsterdam. In her diaries, she described what it was like to live through the German occupation of the Netherlands in the Second World War.

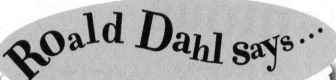

Roald Dahl says...

'I have a passion for teaching kids to become readers, to become comfortable with a book, not daunted. Books shouldn't be daunting, they should be funny, exciting and wonderful; and learning to be a reader gives a terrific advantage.'

Top tip

Roald Dahl always followed the writing advice of top author Ernest Hemingway (1899–1961): when it starts going well, quit.

Cuddly
(and not so cuddly)
creatures

What do *Esio Trot*, *Fantastic Mr Fox* and *The Enormous Crocodile* have in common? Simple – they're all books that star animals instead of humans. Roald Dahl loved animals. He liked dogs, birds, goats and even spiders. But there were exceptions. He hated cats. And he wasn't terribly fond of wasps either. As for snakes, see page 68 to find out what he thought of them.

...a grizzly bear

Move slowly away. Do not run. (Better still, don't attract one in the first place. Make sure all food and smelly things are stored in airtight containers.)

...a shark

Get out of the water as soon as possible, as calmly as you can. (Sharks are attracted by splashing.) But if you can't escape, hit the shark on the nose with a spear, a camera or whatever you are holding. Don't use your bare hands – they are not as easy to replace.

...a deadly spider

If you can escape, do. If you've been bitten, squeeze the wound. The blood will help to wash out the poison. Clean the bite with soap and water. Go to a hospital, especially if you have breathing difficulties or chest pain.

. . . a snake

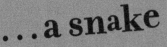

If you are attacked by an anaconda, do not run. (There's no point – the snake is faster than you.) Lie flat on the ground with your arms tucked in and legs straight. Do not panic, even if the snake slithers all over your body. When it starts to swallow your legs, still do not panic. Wait until the anaconda has reached your knees, then reach down and use your knife to slice the snake's head off. (If you do not have a knife, now might be the time to panic.)

. . . a Tyrannosaurus rex

Run or hide! Whatever, you should stay out of reach of those deadly teeth. The Tyrannosaurus rex was most definitely not a vegetarian.

. . . a diplodocus

Just sit back and enjoy the show. This was a total pussy cat of a dinosaur – experts think that it stripped leaves from branches rather than ripping meat from bones. You might want to watch out for those feet, though. The diplodocus was no lightweight.

Earth time

The history of our planet is divided into handy chunks of time, called eras. If ever you want to show off, just drop a few of these into a conversation.

ERA 🌎	WHEN WAS IT? 🕐
Cenozoic	65.5 mya (million years ago) to now
Mesozoic	251–65.5 mya
Paleozoic	542–251 mya
Neoproterozoic	1,000–542 mya
Mesoproterozoic	1,600–1,000 mya
Paleoproterozoic	2,500–1,600 mya
Neoarchean	2,800–2,500 mya
Mesoarchean	3,200–2,800 mya
Paleoarchean	3,600–3,200 mya
Eoarchean	3,800–3,600 mya

The Eoarchean era was preceded by the Hadean eon, which began 4,500 mya when the Earth was formed.

Perhaps the most famous of these eras is the Mesozoic, which is also known as the 'Age of Dinosaurs'. This can be split up into three smaller chunks of time.

Triassic	About 251–200 mya
Jurassic	About 200–145 mya
Cretaceous	About 145–65 mya

Heroic animals

Bamse was a very special St Bernard dog who lived on the Norwegian ship *Thorodd*. During the Second World War, he saved not one but two sailors – one from a knife attack and another from drowning. In 2006, sixty-two years after his death, the dog was awarded the PDSA gold medal for exceptional acts of gallantry and devotion to duty. It's the animals' version of the George Cross.

The Dickin Medal is known as the animals' Victoria Cross. Between 1943 and 1949, it was awarded to thirty-two pigeons, eighteen dogs, three horses and one cat, because of their brave actions during the Second World War. There are so many pigeons because they were used to carry messages.

The following animals have all won the Dickin Medal for Gallantry:

PADDY (1944): a carrier pigeon who made the fastest recorded crossing of the Channel to deliver messages from Normandy for D-Day in the Second World War.

JUDY (1946): a ship's dog who alerted crew to approaching aircraft. She was also the only animal officially registered as a prisoner of war.

SIMON (1949): a ship's cat on HMS Amethyst during the Chinese civil war. Despite being injured by shellfire, he killed off a rat infestation.

ROSELLE (2002): a guide dog who led her blind owner and a woman blinded by debris from the World Trade Center during the attacks of 9/11.

SAM (2003): a dog serving with the Royal Canadian Regiment in Bosnia. He disarmed a gunman and guarded refugees against a hostile crowd.

Roald Dahl's pets

Chopper, Roald Dahl's brown-and-white Jack Russell terrier was the last dog he ever owned and he was very naughty. Chopper dined like a lord, feasting on oysters, caviar, Smarties and, every now and again, dog food.

Roald Dahl bought and trained his own greyhounds. Snailbox Lady was the first greyhound.

Did you know?

A cockroach can live for a week without its head.

Top ten dogs' names in 2006

1. Molly
2. Jack
3. Holly
4. Max
5. Buster
6. Lucy
7. Jake
8. Barney
9. Charlie
10. Sam

Top ten cats' names in 2006

1. Molly
2. Felix
3. Smudge
4. Sooty
5. Tigger
6. Charlie
7. Alfie
8. Oscar
9. Millie
10. Misty

The most popular UK dog breeds in 2006

Top dog is the Labrador, followed by cocker spaniels, then springer spaniels. In fourth place is the Alsatian.

Only three members of Roald Dahl's family ever appeared in his books. And only one of those was human. His granddaughter Sophie starred in *The BFG*. The parrot in *Matilda* was named Chopper, after his Jack Russell terrier. And Alma the goat was in *George's Marvellous Medicine*.

Roald Dahl says...

'We have a pair of swallows that have built their nest in exactly the same place on a wooden beam in the tool shed for the past six years, and it is amazing to me how they fly off thousands of miles to North Africa in the autumn with their young and then six months later they find their way back to the same tool shed at Gipsy House, Great Missenden, Bucks. It's a miracle and the brainiest ornithologists in the world still cannot explain how they do it.'

All together now!

Groups of animals are given special names (they're called collective nouns). Some of these names are quite extraordinary. Here's a mixture of some you might know already – and others you probably don't!

A BASK OF CROCODILES
A BROOD OF HENS
A CARAVAN OF CAMELS
A CLAN OF HYENAS
A CRASH OF RHINOCEROSES
A DRAY OF SQUIRRELS
A DROVE OF CATTLE
A FLOCK OF SEAGULLS
A GAGGLE OF GEESE
A HERD OF ANTELOPE
A HOVER OF TROUT
A LEAP OF LEOPARDS
A MURDER OF CROWS
A PARLIAMENT OF OWLS
A PLAGUE OF LOCUSTS
A POD OF DOLPHINS
A QUIVER OF COBRAS
A TROUBLING OF GOLDFINCHES
A WATCH OF NIGHTINGALES
AN UNKINDNESS OF RAVENS

9

Money, Money, Money

Then one afternoon, walking back home with the icy wind in his face (and incidentally feeling hungrier than he had ever felt before), his eye was caught suddenly by something silvery lying in the gutter, in the snow. Charlie stepped off the kerb and bent down to examine it. Part of it was buried under the snow, but he saw at once what it was.

It was a fifty pence piece!

From *Charlie and the Chocolate Factory*

Shells, beads and tobacco leaves

Charlie Bucket was thrilled to find a fifty pence coin in the snow. But, if he'd lived in China long ago, he would have been just as delighted to find a cowrie shell – the local currency. Sadly, he wouldn't have been able to buy a **WONKA'S WHIPPLE-SCRUMPTIOUS FUDGEMALLOW DELIGHT**, as these hadn't been invented then. Here are more strange currencies from throughout history . . .

Wampum were beautiful beads made from oblong clamshells, which Native Americans once used as money in North America. Black wampum beads were worth twice as much as white ones.

People from the Micronesian island of Yap quarried **limestone rocks** and then made them into enormous coins – the bigger the rock coin, the greater the value.

Early American colonists used **tobacco leaves** and **deer hide** as money.

Europeans once used **peppercorns** to pay for their shopping. And Romans used **salt**.

Money slang

People often use strange words to describe different amounts of money. How many of these have you heard?

£1 = a quid, a nicker

£5 = a fiver

£10 = a tenner

£25 = a pony, a macaroni

£50 = a nifty

£100 = a tonne, a one-er

£500 = a monkey

£1,000 = a grand, a 'k'

Other words for money

DOSH Dough Filthy lucre

READIES

Lolly Moola

WONGA Spondulicks

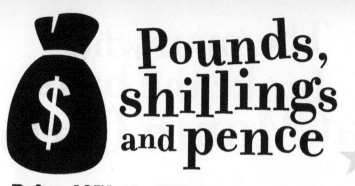

Pounds, shillings and pence

Before 1971, the UK's money was very different. If you were lucky, here's what you would have had jangling around in your pocket – and how much it would be worth now.

Old money	New money
Farthing	0.104p
Halfpenny	0.208p
Penny (a copper)	0.417p
Threepence (a thrupp'ny bit)	1.25p
Sixpence (a tanner)	2.5p
Shilling (a bob)	5p
Florin	10p
Half crown (two shillings and sixpence)	12.5p
Crown	25p
Half sovereign	50p
Sovereign	£1
Guinea (twenty-one shillings)	£1.05

The man who broke the bank at Monte Carlo

Charles Wells (1841-1926) was a con man and a gambler. In 1891, he took £4,000 of his ill-gotten gains to Monte Carlo – the gambler's paradise. There, he broke the bank over and over again. (When someone 'breaks the bank', this means that they win more than the money that is on the gambling table.) In one eleven-hour stint, Wells broke the bank an unbelievable twelve times. And how did he do it? According to Charles Wells, it was pure luck. By 1892, he had become so famous that someone wrote a song about him. It was called 'The man who broke the bank at Monte Carlo'.

What's the quickest way to double your money?

Fold it.

What did Roald Dahl like to spend his money on?

Roald Dahl loved art. He loved learning about it, buying and selling it. But most of all he loved looking at it. If a picture caught his eye, he would snap it up – even if it was far too expensive ... then he'd sometimes have to sell it again when he was broke. And that's where the money came in. To Roald Dahl, one of the best things about making it as an author was that he could afford to keep his pictures.

RD♥ART

10

More likes and dislikes and wonders and pops that whizz that couldn't be squeezed into the other nine chapters

It's hard to believe, but there are people who don't know what a whizzpopper is. It's true! Worse still, they don't know how to whizzpop. Shocking, isn't it?

More things that
ROald Dahl liked

1. Orchids
2. Paintings
3. Chocolate
4. Conkers
5. Racing greyhounds
6. Medical inventions
7. Breeding homing budgies
8. Golf
9. Onions
10. Antiques

And the thing he liked most of all in people:

'I think probably kindness is my number one attribute in a human being. I'll put it before any of the things like courage or bravery or generosity or anything else.'

Le Pétomane

At the end of the nineteenth century, Joseph Pujol – otherwise known as **Le Pétomane** – was the highest paid celebrity in France. And what was his claim to fame? Was he a leading actor? A world-famous singer? A royal prince? No, none of these. Instead, Le Pétomane was known for one thing. His horrible habit of whizzpopping! That's right! To put it bluntly, he was the premiere pumper throughout the whole of Europe and was so skilled, in fact, that not only could he summon up a whizzpop at will, but he could also bottom-burp tunes (which his paying audience would gamely sing along to) and even play the flute with his bum!

What causes whizzpops?

Flatulence is the technical term for a whizzpop, and is caused by a combination of air getting swallowed while eating, as well as gases produced when food is being digested in the stomach. Some foods cause more gases than others, which is why, after a plate of baked beans, you're more likely to, ahem, suffer from flatulence.

The seven wonders of the ancient world

This list of must-see wonders was compiled so long ago that most of them have fallen down or burned down. The only wonder still standing is the Great Pyramid of Giza, in Egypt. It was once the world's tallest building.

☆ Great Pyramid of Giza

☆ Hanging Gardens of Babylon

☆ Temple of Artemis at Ephesus

☆ Statue of Zeus at Olympia

☆ Mausoleum of Maussollos at Harlicarnassus

☆ Colossus of Rhodes

☆ Lighthouse of Alexandria

The seven wonders of the modern world

There are so many wonders in the modern world that people have found it hard to agree which are the seven most wonderful. The American Society of Civil Engineers compiled a list of seven man-made wonders . . .

☆ Channel Tunnel (the 50.5 km undersea rail tunnel between England and France)

☆ CN Tower (the world's tallest freestanding structure – Toronto, Canada)

☆ Empire State Building (the world's tallest building from 1931 to 1972 – New York City, USA)

☆ Golden Gate Bridge (once the largest suspension bridge in the world – San Francisco, USA)

☆ Itaipu Dam (a hydro-electric dam – Paraná River, South America)

☆ Netherlands North Sea Protection Works (dams, sluices, locks, dykes and storm surge barriers built to protect the Netherlands from the sea)

☆ Panama Canal (a ship canal that connects the Atlantic and Pacific Oceans via the isthmus of Panama, South America)

... while CNN compiled a list of natural wonders.

☆ Grand Canyon (Arizona, USA)

☆ Great Barrier Reef (Australia)

☆ Rio de Janeiro harbour (Brazil)

☆ Mount Everest (Nepal/China)

☆ Polar Aurora (bright, colourful lights in the night sky at the North and South poles)

☆ Parícutin volcano (Mexico)

☆ Victoria Falls (Zambia/Zimbabwe)

Famous people's **favourite** children's books

Zoë Ball (TV and radio presenter)

Where the Wild Things Are
by Maurice Sendak

Tony Blair (ex-Prime Minister)

The Lord of the Rings
by J. R. R. Tolkein

Roald Dahl (author)

Mr Midshipman Easy
by Captain Frederick Marryat

Jamie Foxx (actor)
Green Eggs and Ham
by Dr Seuss

Dick King-Smith (author)
Tarka the Otter
by Henry Williamson

J. K. Rowling (author)
The Little White Horse
by Elizabeth Goudge

Steven Spielberg (director)
Treasure Island
by Robert Louis Stevenson

Emma Watson (actor)
Roald Dahl's books!

20 questions

WARNING: This gloriumptiously difficult quiz is for dedicated Dahl fans only. Proceed at your own peril.

1 Which one of these books is not a Roald Dahl story?
a) *The Magic Finger*
b) *A Piece of Cake*
c) *The Raspberry-Ripple Ice Cream*

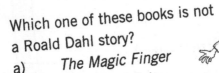

2 Quentin Blake illustrated all but one of Roald Dahl's children's books. Which was it?

3 What did Roald Dahl almost lose in a car accident?

4 Was Roald Dahl a good speller or a bad speller?

5 Who was a 'great big greedy nincompoop'?

 6 What did Roald Dahl fly during the Second World War?

a) A helicopter.
b) A balloon.
c) A fighter plane.

 7 What is the sequel to *Charlie and the Chocolate Factory*?

 8 If Roald Dahl hadn't been an author, what would he have liked to be?

 9 Who is the 'Boy' in the title of Roald Dahl's book?

10 What does BFG stand for?

11 Who played Willy Wonka in the 2005 film of *Charlie and the Chocolate Factory*?

12 Which country did Roald Dahl's parents come from?

13 What was the name of Matilda's nice teacher . . .?

14 . . . and what was the name of her spiteful headmistress?

15 What is frobscottle?

16 What type of music did Roald Dahl like best?
a) Classical music.
b) Jazz music.
c) Pop music.

17 Roald Dahl wrote the screenplay for the James Bond film *You Only Live Twice*. **True or false?**

 18 Which grandmother is Roald Dahl's kindest, nicest character? Is it the one from *George's Marvellous Medicine* or the one from *The Witches*?

 19 Did Roald Dahl have a middle name?

 20 Where is the Roald Dahl Museum and Story Centre?

Answers on page 145

How did you score?

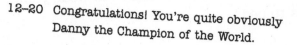

12–20 Congratulations! You're quite obviously Danny the Champion of the World.

6–11 Well done! You're as clever as Fantastic Mr Fox.

0–5 Oh dear. You're a Twit.

Totally true laws

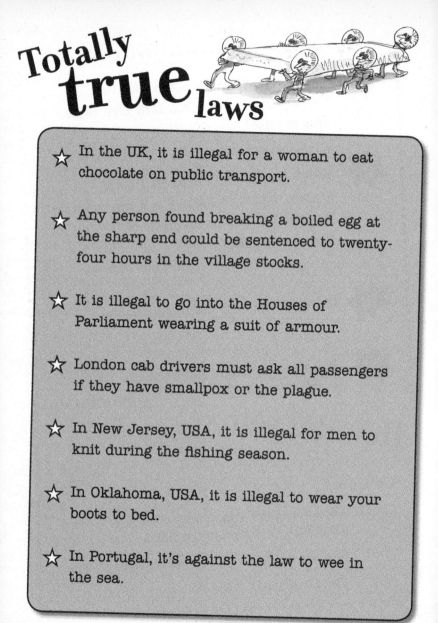

★ In the UK, it is illegal for a woman to eat chocolate on public transport.

★ Any person found breaking a boiled egg at the sharp end could be sentenced to twenty-four hours in the village stocks.

★ It is illegal to go into the Houses of Parliament wearing a suit of armour.

★ London cab drivers must ask all passengers if they have smallpox or the plague.

★ In New Jersey, USA, it is illegal for men to knit during the fishing season.

★ In Oklahoma, USA, it is illegal to wear your boots to bed.

★ In Portugal, it's against the law to wee in the sea.

And, finally,

Roald Dahl says...

'Watch with glittering eyes the whole world around you because the greatest secrets are always hidden in the most unlikely places. Those who don't believe in magic will never find it.'

Answers

Who's who? pages 20–21

It is, of course, a witch!

Fictional baddies pages 36–37

Bill Sikes (*Oliver Twist* by Charles Dickens)

Captain James Hook (*Peter Pan* by J. M. Barrie)

Cruella De Vil (*The Hundred and One Dalmatians* by Dodie Smith)

Farmer Boggis, Farmer Bunce and Farmer Bean (*Fantastic Mr Fox* by Roald Dahl)

Long John Silver (*Treasure Island* by Robert Louis Stevenson)

Lord Voldemort (*Harry Potter and the Philosopher's Stone* by J. K. Rowling)

Professor James Moriarty (Sherlock Holmes novels by Sir Arthur Conan Doyle)

Sauron, the Dark Lord (*Lord of the Rings* by J. R. R. Tolkein)

Shere Khan (*The Jungle Book* by Rudyard Kipling)

The White Witch (*The Lion, the Witch and the Wardrobe* by C. S. Lewis)

The Wicked Witch of the West (*The Wonderful Wizard of Oz* by L. Frank Baum)

George's Marvellous Quiz page 62

The fake ingredients are: cat ointment for cats with mange, nits, fleas and very bad tempers; a tin of cabbage soup; castor oil; the mould from a three-week-old cheese sandwich; a Brussels sprouts smoothie.

Topsy-turvy quiz question page 67

Mr and Mrs Twit

Fictional food page 80

Tender juicy lettuce leaves (*Esio Trot*)

Snozzcumbers and frobscottle (*The BFG*)

Squiggly spaghetti (*The Twits*)

Chicken, turkey, goose and duck (*Fantastic Mr Fox*)

Swudge – edible grass made of soft, minty sugar
(*Charlie and the Chocolate Factory*)

Likes and dislikes pages 82–83

1. c) Roald Dahl's favourite colour was yellow. He wrote all of his books
on yellow paper and he used yellow pencils too. 2. b) Although he loved
Christmas as a child, the grown-up Roald Dahl hated it. He thought that
Christmas made people spend money on presents that they couldn't
afford to buy. 3. a) Caviar! Did you know that although Roald Dahl loved
chocolate, he really didn't like chocolate-flavoured things? 4. a) He would
use the mushrooms he collected to make mushrooms on toast. 5. c) His
favourite composer was Beethoven.

Even sillier scribbles page 96

The Twits, Going Solo, Boy, The Witches, Esio Trot

20 questions pages 138–141

1. c) 2. The Minpins. 3. His nose. 4. A very bad speller. 5. Augustus Gloop.
6. c) 7. *Charlie and the Great Glass Elevator.* 8. A doctor. 9. Roald Dahl! 10.
Big Friendly Giant. 11. Johnny Depp. 12. Norway. 13. Miss Honey. 14. Miss
Trunchbull. 15. A fizzy drink. 16. a) 17. True. 18. The grandmother from
The Witches. 19. No. 20. Great Missenden, Buckinghamshire.

Find out more about your favourite
Roald Dahl books with these delicious
details of how they came about.

Charlie and the Chocolate Factory

Roald Dahl found *Charlie and the Chocolate Factory* one
of the most difficult books to write. His first draft of
the story included fifteen horrible children. His nephew
Nicholas read it and said it was rotten and boring, so Roald
Dahl realized he needed to rewrite it!

The idea for Charlie came from Roald Dahl's schooldays,
when he and other classmates were occasionally asked by
Cadbury's to test newly invented chocolate bars. He used
to dream of inventing his own famous chocolate bar that
would win the praise of Mr Cadbury himself.

The Twits

Roald Dahl kept an old school exercise book in which
he wrote all the ideas for his stories. Some of the ideas
stayed in there for twenty or more years before he came
to incorporate them into books. The idea for *The Twits*
simply said 'do something against beards'. Roald Dahl
was not a fan of beards and said he never
understood why a man wanted to hide
his face behind a big bushy beard.

Danny the Champion of the World

Danny the Champion of the World is one of Roald Dahl's only books that is based on first-hand experience. When he moved to Buckinghamshire, he became friends with a man called Claude who worked in the local butcher's. Claude had a passion for poaching and the two of them would sometimes sneak into the local woods in the dead of night to catch pheasants. Roald Dahl never caught a single bird, but enjoyed the thrill of the experience. Like Danny, Roald's own children learned to drive at a very young age. He taught his daughter Ophelia to drive when she was only ten years old! The caravan in this story is based on the sky-blue caravan that sits in Roald Dahl's garden.

The BFG

Roald Dahl invented the story of the BFG for his own children. He would sometimes put a ladder up to their window when they were in bed and stir the curtains or even push through a bamboo cane as if the BFG himself were really outside blowing dreams into their bedroom. The BFG's friend, Sophie, is named after a real Sophie, Roald's granddaughter. She is the only family member whose name he used for a character in one of his books. Of all the characters he created, the BFG was probably his favourite, as he valued kindness above all other qualities in life.

Matilda

Roald Dahl remembered what it was like to live in a child's world and kept this in mind when he wrote *Matilda*. He once said that in order to see life from a child's point of view you had to get down on your hands and knees and look up at the adults towering above you, telling you what to do. Matilda's triumph over the nasty adults in her life is based on this theory.

George's Marvellous Medicine

Roald Dahl had a little brown and white Jack Russell terrier called Chopper. Little did anyone think he'd be inspired to write Chopper's bottom into this book!

Roald Dahl wrote all his children's books from a specially built writing hut in the apple orchard of his house in Great Missenden. It was so private that he never let anyone in to clean it and it gathered dust for more than fifteen years! It was full of litter and spiders' webs – he adored spiders.

The Witches

Just like the grandmother in this story, Roald Dahl's parents were Norwegian. He spent many happy holidays in Norway and much of the Norwegian details in the book are taken from his childhood experiences. The grandmother is actually based on his own mother.

Roald Dahl's children had fifty different-coloured glass balls hanging from their bedroom ceiling. Their father told them that they were witch balls and if any witch came near in the night she would flee in fright at her ghastly reflection in the balls.

James and the Giant Peach

James and the Giant Peach was Roald Dahl's second book for children. He wrote it in New York in the winter of 1960 after a stretch of seventeen years in which he had written only short stories for adults. Roald Dahl's baby son, Theo, had a terrible accident while Roald was writing this book, and he said that being able to disappear into this fantasy world for a few hours each day helped him through the crisis. Today, happily, both Theo and James are very much alive and well.

Fantastic Mr Fox

Roald Dahl's garden outside his Georgian house in Great Missenden, Buckinghamshire, backed on to fields and a wood. At the top of the lane stood a fifty-year-old beech tree and this became the setting for *Fantastic Mr Fox*. Of all his books, Dahl thought this to be his best balanced, with everything in the right place.

Charlie and the Great Glass Elevator

Just as Charlie and his friends are invited to meet the President of the United States, Roald Dahl also received such an invitation. Eleanor Roosevelt loved his first book, *The Gremlins*, and asked him to dinner at the White House. One day he went for a drive in the country with President Roosevelt and they drove on the wrong side of the road, forcing the other cars off the highway! He became a welcome guest of the President and his wife and even stayed at the weekend retreat, Hyde Park.

SURPRISE

Bet you thought this book had finished.
Well, here's some truly marvellous news – it hasn't! Turn
the page for a whole load of Roald Dahl treats.

YIPPPPEEEE!

GOBBLEFUNK

Roald Dahl loved playing around with words and inventing new ones. In *The BFG* he gave this strange language an even stranger name – Gobblefunk!

BAGGLEPIPES

Bagpipes: famous Scottish wind instrument.

BOGGLEBOX

A school for young children (generally boys).

CRABCRUNCHER

Crabcrunchers live high up on cliffs by the sea. They're very rare.

FROTHBUNGLING

Means stupid.

GLORIUMPTIOUS

Gloriously wonderful.

HUMAN BEAN

This is the name the giants in *The BFG* give to human beings.

Roald Dahl's
SCHOOL REPORTS

In 1929, when he was thirteen, Roald Dahl was sent to boarding school. You would expect him to get wonderful marks in English – but his school reports were *not* good!

My end-of-term reports from this school are of some interest. Here are just four of them, copied word for word from the original documents:

SUMMER TERM, 1930 (aged 14).
English Composition.

"I have never met a boy who so persistently writes the exact opposite of what he means. He seems incapable of marshalling his thoughts on paper."

EASTER TERM, 1931 (aged 15). *English Composition.*
"A persistent muddler. Vocabulary negligible, sentences malconstructed. He reminds me of a camel."

SUMMER TERM, 1932 (aged 16). *English Composition.*
"This boy is an indolent and illiterate member of the class."

AUTUMN TERM, 1932 (aged 17). *English Composition.*
"Consistently idle. Ideas limited."

Little wonder that it never entered my head to become a writer in those days.

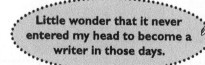

Find out more about Roald Dahl at school in *Boy*.

153

THERE'S MORE TO ROALD DAHL THAN GREAT STORIES...

Did you know that 10% of Roald Dahl's royalties* from this book go to help the work of the Roald Dahl charities?

Roald Dahl's Marvellous Children's Charity aims to raise as much money as possible to make seriously ill children's lives better because it believes that every child has the right to a marvellous life. This marvellous charity helps thousands of children each year in the UK living with serious conditions of the blood and the brain – causes important to Roald Dahl in his lifetime.

Whether by providing nurses, equipment, carers or toys, the charity helps to care for children with conditions including acquired brain injury, epilepsy and blood disorders such as sickle cell disease. Can you do something marvellous to help others?

Find out how at **www.marvellouschildrenscharity.org**

The Roald Dahl Museum and Story Centre, based in Great Missenden just outside London, is in the Buckinghamshire village where Roald Dahl lived and wrote. At the heart of the Museum, created to inspire a love of reading and writing, is his unique archive of letters and manuscripts. As well as two fun-packed biographical galleries, the Museum boasts an interactive Story Centre. It is a place for the family, teachers and their pupils to explore the exciting world of creativity and literacy.

Roald Dahl's Marvellous Children's Charity (RDMCC) is a registered charity no. 1004230.

The Roald Dahl Museum and Story Centre is a registered charity no. 1085853

The Roald Dahl Charitable Trust is a registered charity no. 1119330 and supports the work of RDMCC and RDMSC.

* Donated royalties are net of commission

roalddahlfoundation.org
roalddahlmuseum.org